THE airfryer COOKBOOK

WILLIAMS-SONOMA
test kitchen

photographs Aubrie Pick

weldon**owen**

Contents

Welcome to Airfrying

The Philips Viva Digital Airfryer is an innovative countertop appliance that will revolutionize the way you cook. Its patented design uses hot air flow, of temperatures ranging from 180° to 390°F, to quickly cook delicious, crisp food. Much more than a frying device, the Airfryer can also be used for baking, roasting, and grilling. Using little or no oil, it cooks food that is crisp on the outside and tender on the inside, including such favorites as French fries, pizza, chicken wings, and brownies.

The Rapid Air technology and "starfish" design create a vortex of fast-circulating, super-hot air that cooks food faster and more evenly than a conventional oven. With almost no oil, the Airfryer produces the same crisp exterior found on deep-fried fare and other recipes that require tablespoons of oil, so you can eat healthier without giving up the foods you love.

On the pages that follow, you'll find a primer on how to use the Airfryer to prepare a variety of lightened-up and quick-cooking dishes, from breakfast through dinner. Try the Banana-Walnut Bread (page 21) and Spinach Baked Eggs (page 17) for a weekend brunch. BBQ Chicken (page 33) makes a wonderful weeknight supper, while Thai Red Curry Fish Fillets (page 26) are perfect for easy entertaining. You can even bake Triple-Chocolate Brownies (page 51) and turn out tasty, healthy snacks in the Airfryer, such as Kale Chips (page 45) and Samosas with Cilantro Sauce (page 46). You'll find these and many more foolproof recipes, both savory and sweet, to help you make the most of this innovative tool.

**Digital touch screen
control panel**
with temperatures
ranging from
180° to 390°F

for changing
out accessories

PHILIPS

**Dishwasher-safe
accessories**

390°F	360°F	360°F
12-16 min.	18-25 min.	8-14 min.
360°F	390°F	390°F
15-22 min.	6-10 min.	15-18 min.

Airfryer Primer

Preparing healthier fried, baked, roasted, and grilled foods in the Airfryer is a six-step process. With a bit of practice, you'll discover how easy it is to cook with this amazing appliance.

1   Set the Airfryer on a stable, heat-resistant work surface, or place a thick trivet between the appliance and the surface. Then plug the unit into a wall outlet.

2   Using the touch screen control panel, press the power button on the lower right corner, set the temperature using the up/down arrows, and press the start button on the bottom center of the panel. The set temperature will flash until the temperature is reached; allow at least 3 minutes for preheating.

3   Set the cooking time by pressing the up/down arrows on the touch screen. The unit will automatically shut off once the timer goes off. Set the timer for a few minutes longer than the recipe calls for so you won't have to reset the appliance if the food needs to cook longer. You can change the time or temperature anytime during the cooking process.

4   Carefully remove the hot variety cooking basket or grill pan from the preheated Airfryer. Add the food (placing the baking dish or the double layer rack inside the variety cooking basket, if the recipe calls for it), and then slide the basket or grill pan back into the Airfryer.

5   Unless the recipe directs otherwise, check the food halfway through the cooking time to ensure it is cooking evenly. See Airfryer Tips & Tricks (page 12) for ways to produce evenly cooked food and to prevent overbrowning and smoking.

6   When cooking is complete, carefully remove the food from the Airfryer with tongs or a long-handled spatula. The cooking accessories will be very hot, and opening the appliance may release hot steam.

Airfryer Accessories

The Philips Viva Digital Airfryer comes with an assortment of accessories, and each one creates a unique cooking experience, whether you are baking or grilling.

1 The Variety Cooking Basket with Splatter-Proof Lid

This multiuse cooking basket lets you fry and bake with a minimal amount of oil. The removable splatter-proof lid helps to reduce the speed in which food browns, so food cooks at the same rate, both inside and out. The lid also controls the amount of smoke produced by ingredients with a higher fat content. Both the lid and the bottom of the basket are removable for easy cleanup. (This Airfryer allows you to use the lidless frying basket accessory that comes with older models of the Airfryer.)

2 The Nonstick Baking Dish

This pull-out dish makes baking healthier and faster. Use it for preparing everything from cakes and egg dishes to breads and grains. The nonstick surface releases food effortlessly and ensures easy cleanup.

3 The Nonstick Grill Pan

The grill pan excels at frying, searing, and adding grill marks and a smoky flavor to your favorite foods, while the pierced surface allows excess fat to drip away. Enjoy the results of grilling with almost no oil and without having to fire up an outdoor grill.

4 The Double Layer Rack

This plated-steel rack increases the cooking surface, so you can prepare twice the amount of food. It's excellent for baking or frying burgers, chicken, and even kabobs (four skewers are included with the rack).

1	2
3	4

Airfryer Tips & Tricks

Preparing food with the Airfryer is simple, and these tips for using and caring for your appliance will help you to maximize your cooking experience.

Cooking

The recipes in this book have been developed for use in the Philips Viva Digital Airfryer, but will also work in the Philips Avance XL Digital Airfryer. If using the Avance XL Digital Airfryer, note that cooking times will be about 30 percent faster, so check for doneness a few minutes earlier than indicated in the recipe.

For optimal and even cooking results, do not overfill or overcrowd the cooking accessories. A "max" line on the variety cooking basket illustrates maximum capacity. Leave at least 1 inch of space between items cooked on the grill pan and on the double layer rack, and never stack food. Leave at least 1½ inches of headroom when filling the baking dish to prevent food from bubbling over.

Unless your recipe directs otherwise, remove the cooking accessory once or twice to ensure the food is cooking evenly.

If food is browning too quickly or excess oil or rendered fat is splattering, carefully insert the splatter-proof lid onto the variety cooking basket. The basket will be very hot.

When cooking foods with a higher fat content, such as skin-on chicken pieces or steak, occasionally remove the cooking accessory and drain excess fat from the bottom of the Airfryer. This will prevent smoke from building up.

Some small food items should be gently shaken or turned with tongs midway through cooking.

Cleaning

Clean the Airfryer after each use to remove oil and to prevent smoke from building up the next time you use the appliance. Unplug the Airfryer after you are finished cooking, and let it cool completely. Wipe the outside of the unit with a moist cloth. Remove the cooking accessory and set aside. Thoroughly clean the interior of the appliance with hot, soapy water and a nonabrasive sponge, then let dry completely before storing.

All the accessories are dishwasher safe. Let them cool completely before washing in the dishwasher or with hot, soapy water and a nonabrasive sponge.

French Toast Sticks with Berry Compote

French toast just got a lot more fun with this sweet breakfast finger food. Challah is our favorite, but you can use sliced brioche or other good-quality white bread. Any leftover berry compote is great stirred into yogurt or spooned over ice cream.

In a small saucepan over medium-high heat, combine the berries and 3 tablespoons of the granulated sugar. Bring to a boil, then cook, stirring occasionally, until thickened, about 6 minutes. Stir in the lemon juice. Set the compote aside.

Preheat the Airfryer to 390°F. Lightly oil the double layer rack.

In a bowl, whisk together the half-and-half, egg, vanilla, cinnamon, and the remaining 2 tablespoons granulated sugar. Dip half of the challah strips in the mixture to coat all sides and place in a single layer on the prepared double layer rack. Carefully set the rack inside the variety cooking basket and insert the basket into the Airfryer. Cook, uncovered, until the French toast sticks are browned, about 8 minutes, turning them twice midway through cooking. Transfer to a plate and repeat with the remaining challah strips.

Dust the French toast sticks with confectioners' sugar and serve the berry compote alongside.

SERVES 4

1 bag (10 oz) frozen mixed berries, thawed

5 tablespoons granulated sugar

2 teaspoons fresh lemon juice

Vegetable oil, for greasing

½ cup half-and-half

1 large egg

1 teaspoon pure vanilla extract

¼ teaspoon ground cinnamon

½ loaf challah, cut into 4½-by-1-by-¾-inch strips

Confectioners' sugar, for dusting

Chicken Apple Pigs in a Blanket

These puff pastry–wrapped sausages are an excellent addition to a weekend breakfast spread, especially when paired with simple scrambled eggs. For a more savory dish, use your favorite smoked chicken sausage flavor, such as sundried tomato or roasted garlic.

Preheat the Airfryer to 390°F.

On a lightly floured surface, roll out the puff pastry into an 8-by-12-inch rectangle. Cut into 4 strips lengthwise, then into 3 sections crosswise to create twelve 2-by-4-inch rectangles. Cut each rectangle diagonally into 2 triangles.

Spread ¼ teaspoon mustard on each triangle and sprinkle with 1 teaspoon cheese. Place a piece of sausage on the base of a triangle and roll the pastry up around it. Transfer to a baking sheet. Repeat with the remaining pastry, mustard, cheese, and sausages. Brush the tops of the pastries with the egg wash.

Carefully place 6 pastry-wrapped sausages in the variety cooking basket. Set the double layer rack inside the basket and place 6 pastry-wrapped sausages on the rack. Insert the basket into the Airfryer. Cook, uncovered, until the pastry is evenly browned, about 8 minutes. Transfer to a platter. Repeat with the remaining 12 pastry-wrapped sausages.

SERVES 6

All-purpose flour, for dusting

1 frozen puff pastry sheet, thawed

2 tablespoons whole-grain mustard

½ cup grated Cheddar cheese

3 links chicken apple sausage, each quartered lengthwise and halved crosswise

1 large egg beaten with 1 teaspoon water

Spinach Baked Eggs

The Airfryer cooks eggs quickly and easily. Here, eggs are baked with spinach and a touch of cream to create a delicious breakfast in no time. If you like, substitute chopped chard leaves for the spinach, and increase the cooking time by 3 minutes.

Preheat the Airfryer to 360°F. Lightly oil the bottom and sides of the nonstick baking dish.

In a large sauté pan over medium heat, warm the oil. Add the shallots and garlic and cook, stirring occasionally, until translucent, about 1 minute. Add the spinach and ¼ cup water and cook, stirring occasionally, until the spinach is wilted, about 2 minutes. Add the cream and a pinch of salt and cook until the cream has reduced, 1–2 minutes.

Transfer the spinach mixture to the nonstick baking dish. Using the back of a spoon, create 2 wells in the spinach mixture, each 3–4 inches in diameter. Carefully crack 1 egg into each well. Carefully place the baking dish in the variety cooking basket, cover with the splatter-proof lid, and insert the basket into the Airfryer. Cook until the egg whites are set and the yolks are still runny, 8–10 minutes.

Season the eggs with salt and pepper and serve right away.

SERVES 2

1 tablespoon olive oil, plus more for greasing

2 shallots, diced

2 cloves garlic, minced

½ lb baby spinach

2 tablespoons heavy cream

Kosher salt and freshly ground pepper

2 large eggs

Mushroom-Chard Frittata with Goat Cheese

This hearty vegetable-packed frittata makes a colorful centerpiece for a weekend brunch. Feel free to substitute white mushrooms or even wild mushrooms for the cremini and other types of tender greens, like spinach, for the chard.

Preheat the Airfryer to 360°F. Lightly oil the bottom and sides of the nonstick baking dish.

In a nonstick frying pan over medium-high heat, warm 1 tablespoon of the oil. Add the mushrooms and thyme, season with salt and pepper, and cook, stirring occasionally, until the mushrooms are lightly browned, about 4 minutes. Transfer to a bowl.

Reduce the heat to medium and warm the remaining 1 tablespoon oil. Add the onion and cook, stirring occasionally, until softened, about 4 minutes. Add the chard and cook, stirring occasionally, until wilted, 3–4 minutes. Transfer to the bowl with the mushrooms.

In a large bowl, whisk the eggs until blended and season with salt and pepper. Stir in the vegetables and cheese. Pour the egg mixture into the prepared baking dish. Carefully place the baking dish in the variety cooking basket and insert the basket into the Airfryer. Cook, uncovered, until the frittata just begins to brown, about 7 minutes. Remove the basket, cover with the splatter-proof lid, and cook until the center of the frittata is set, about 15 minutes longer.

Invert the frittata onto a plate and flip right side up. Sprinkle with the parsley, then slice and serve.

SERVES 2–4

2 tablespoons olive oil, plus more for greasing

¼ lb cremini mushrooms, brushed clean and sliced

½ teaspoon chopped fresh thyme

Kosher salt and freshly ground pepper

½ red onion, diced

½ bunch Swiss chard, stemmed and leaves cut into ¼-inch-wide ribbons

4 large eggs

1 oz goat cheese, crumbled

1 teaspoon chopped fresh flat-leaf parsley

Banana-Walnut Bread

This is a great way to use up bananas that might be too ripe for eating out of hand. Using very ripe bananas is the key to making a luscious banana bread—the riper they are, the sweeter they become. As your bananas ripen, store them in the freezer until ready to use.

Preheat the Airfryer to 330°F. Spray the bottom and sides of the nonstick baking dish with nonstick cooking spray.

In a medium bowl, stir together the flour, baking powder, salt, and baking soda.

In a large bowl, mash the bananas with a fork. Add the sugar, oil, egg, and vanilla and whisk until well blended. Add the flour mixture and whisk just until blended. Fold in the walnuts.

Scrape the batter into the prepared baking dish, spreading it evenly with a rubber spatula. Carefully place the baking dish in the variety cooking basket, cover with the splatter-proof lid, and insert the basket into the Airfryer. Bake until a toothpick inserted into the center of the bread comes out with a few crumbs clinging to it, about 30 minutes.

Remove the baking dish from the Airfryer, place on a wire rack, and let the bread cool for 10 minutes. Invert the bread onto a cutting board and flip right side up. Cut the bread and serve warm or at room temperature with honey and butter, if desired.

SERVES 4

1 cup all-purpose flour

1 teaspoon baking powder

¼ teaspoon table salt

¼ teaspoon baking soda

2 very ripe bananas, peeled

⅓ cup sugar

3 tablespoons vegetable oil

1 egg

1 teaspoon pure vanilla extract

¾ cup walnuts, roughly chopped

Honey and butter, for serving (optional)

Chicken Strips with Honey-Dijon Sauce

These crispy chicken strips will be a hit with kids and adults alike. Using potato chips instead of bread crumbs to coat the chicken adds both flavor and extra crunch. Instead of the mustard sauce, you can serve your favorite barbecue sauce alongside.

Preheat the Airfryer to 390°F. Lightly oil the variety cooking basket and the double layer rack.

Butterfly the chicken breasts and cut each into 9 strips, about 4 inches long and 1 inch wide. Place the potato chips in a shallow bowl. Roll the chicken strips in the chips, pressing firmly so they adhere, and transfer to a large plate.

Carefully place 9 chicken strips in a single layer in the prepared variety cooking basket. Set the prepared double layer rack inside the basket and place the remaining 9 chicken strips on the rack. Insert the basket into the Airfryer. Cook, uncovered, until the coating is crisp and the chicken is opaque, about 15 minutes. Transfer the chicken to a platter.

Meanwhile, in a small bowl, stir together the mustard and honey. Serve the sauce with the chicken strips.

SERVES 4

Vegetable oil, for greasing

2 skinless, boneless chicken breast halves, about ½ lb each

1½ cups crushed salted potato chips

2 tablespoons Dijon mustard

1 tablespoon honey

Asian Meatball Hoagies with Spicy Mayonnaise

Tuck these flavorful Asian meatballs inside hoagie rolls with spicy mayonnaise, julienned carrots, and fresh cilantro to make the perfect sandwich. They are also terrific served on their own with a big salad or atop a bed of steamed rice.

Preheat the Airfryer to 390°F.

In a bowl, stir together the bread crumbs and milk. Let stand for 5 minutes. Add the ground beef, egg, garlic, ginger, sesame oil, green onions, soy sauce, and ½ teaspoon salt and use your hands to mix the ingredients gently but thoroughly. Form the mixture into 12 equal-sized meatballs and place on a plate.

Carefully place 6 of the meatballs on the nonstick grill pan and insert the pan into the Airfryer. Cook until the meatballs are browned on the exterior and no longer pink in the center, about 10 minutes, turning them over halfway through cooking. Transfer the meatballs to a plate. Repeat with the remaining 6 meatballs.

Meanwhile, in a small bowl, stir together the mayonnaise, chili garlic sauce, and honey.

To assemble each sandwich, spread about 1 tablespoon of the spicy mayonnaise on the inside of a hoagie roll and fill with 3 meatballs. Garnish with carrots and cilantro.

SERVES 4

⅓ cup dried bread crumbs

2 tablespoons whole milk

1 lb ground beef

1 large egg, lightly beaten

2 cloves garlic, minced

1 teaspoon minced fresh ginger

2 teaspoons sesame oil

2 green onions, white and tender green parts only, finely chopped

1 tablespoon soy sauce

Kosher salt

3 tablespoons mayonnaise

1 tablespoon chili garlic sauce

1 teaspoon honey

4 hoagie rolls, split

Julienned carrots and chopped fresh cilantro, for serving

Thai Red Curry Fish Fillets

The ease and simplicity of this comforting curried fish recipe belies its impressive flavor and appearance. Steamed jasmine rice and sautéed snow peas are the perfect accompaniments for a quick weeknight supper.

Preheat the Airfryer to 390°F.

Season the fish fillets with salt. In a small bowl, stir together the curry paste and coconut milk. Spread the mixture evenly over the flesh side of the fillets.

Lightly brush the nonstick grill pan with oil. Carefully place the fish, skin side down, on the pan and insert the pan into the Airfryer. Cook until the fish is opaque and flakes easily with a fork, about 8 minutes. Transfer the fish to a plate, sprinkle with the cilantro, and serve with lime wedges.

SERVES 2

2 firm-fleshed white fish fillets, such as sea bass or halibut, about 6 oz each and 1 inch thick

Kosher salt

1½ teaspoons Thai red curry paste

1 tablespoon coconut milk

Vegetable oil, for greasing

1 teaspoon finely chopped fresh cilantro

Lime wedges, for serving

Cheesy Baked Rigatoni

Who doesn't love a cheesy baked pasta dish, especially one that takes less than 30 minutes to cook? The bread crumbs on top add great texture and crunch. Serve this homey favorite with a simple green salad.

Preheat the Airfryer to 390°F. Lightly oil the bottom and sides of the nonstick baking dish.

Bring a large pot of salted water to a boil over high heat. Add the pasta and cook until al dente, about 12 minutes. Drain well and transfer to a large bowl. Stir in the marinara sauce and cheese. Transfer to the prepared baking dish.

In a small bowl, toss together the bread crumbs, oil, and ¼ teaspoon salt until combined. Sprinkle evenly over the pasta. Carefully place the baking dish in the variety cooking basket and insert the basket into the Airfryer. Cook, uncovered, until the cheese is melted and the bread crumbs are crisp and golden brown, about 12 minutes. If the crumbs start getting too dark partway through cooking, remove the basket, cover with the splatter-proof lid, and continue cooking.

Using a spatula or serving spoon, divide the pasta among 2 bowls and serve right away.

SERVES 2

1 tablespoon olive oil, plus more for greasing

Kosher salt

½ lb rigatoni

1 cup marinara sauce

1 cup shredded mozzarella cheese

¾ cup fresh bread crumbs

Sriracha-Honey Wings

Airfrying chicken wings gives them a light, crisp texture without using any oil. Toss them with a sweet and spicy Sriracha-honey sauce and serve creamy blue cheese dip alongside and you've got a delicious appetizer that is ready in no time.

Preheat the Airfryer to 360°F.

Carefully place half of the chicken wings in the variety cooking basket and insert the basket into the Airfryer. Cook, uncovered, turning the wings with tongs 2 or 3 times during cooking, until the skin is browned and crisp, 26–28 minutes. Repeat with the remaining wings.

Meanwhile, in a small saucepan over medium-high heat, combine the honey, Sriracha, soy sauce, butter, and lime juice. Bring to a boil, then reduce the heat to medium-low, and simmer until the sauce has reduced slightly, 2–3 minutes.

Transfer the wings to a large bowl, add the sauce, and toss to coat. Transfer to a platter and sprinkle cilantro leaves on top. Serve right away with blue cheese dip.

SERVES 4

2 lb chicken wings, tips removed and wings cut into drummettes and flats

½ cup honey

¼ cup Sriracha chili sauce

3 tablespoons soy sauce

2 tablespoons unsalted butter

Juice of 1 lime

Fresh cilantro leaves, for serving

Blue cheese dip, for serving

English Muffin Pizzas

These individual pizzas are a great kid-friendly lunch option, especially when served with vegetable sticks or a small green salad. Add different toppings if you like, such as sautéed mushrooms or cooked, crumbled sweet Italian sausage.

Preheat the Airfryer to 390°F.

Spread the marinara sauce on the English muffin halves, dividing evenly. Sprinkle with the cheese and top with the pepperoni.

Carefully place 1 pizza in the variety cooking basket. Set the double layer rack inside the basket and place 1 pizza on the rack. Insert the basket into the Airfryer. Cook, uncovered, until the cheese is melted and lightly browned, about 6 minutes. Transfer to a plate. Repeat with the remaining 2 pizzas.

SERVES 2–4

6 tablespoons marinara sauce

2 English muffins, halved

½ cup shredded mozzarella cheese

2 tablespoons finely diced pepperoni slices

BBQ Chicken

Here, chicken drumsticks are first rubbed with a spice blend that includes paprika and brown sugar. Then partway through cooking, they're slathered with store-bought barbecue sauce. Simple and delicious, this chicken tastes almost like it just came off the grill.

Preheat the Airfryer to 390°F.

In a small bowl, stir together the paprika, garlic powder, 1 teaspoon salt, the brown sugar, and cayenne. Rub the spice mixture evenly over the chicken.

Carefully place half of the chicken in the variety cooking basket. Set the double layer rack inside the basket and place the remaining chicken on the rack. Insert the basket into the Airfryer. Cook, uncovered, for 20 minutes, rotating the chicken between the basket and rack halfway through cooking. Remove the chicken from the Airfryer and brush with some of the barbecue sauce. Return to the Airfryer and cook until an instant-read thermometer inserted into the thickest part of a drumstick, away from the bone, registers 170°F, 5–10 minutes longer.

Transfer the chicken to a platter and serve right away with the remaining barbecue sauce alongside.

SERVES 4

1 tablespoon smoked sweet paprika

1 teaspoon roasted garlic powder

Kosher salt

1 teaspoon light brown sugar

⅛ teaspoon cayenne pepper

6 chicken drumsticks, about 2 lb total weight

1½ cups barbecue sauce

Beef & Vegetable Skewers

With tender steak and fresh summer vegetables, these are a healthy and colorful option for a weeknight family dinner. Serve these quick-cooking skewers on their own or paired with couscous. They're also excellent wrapped in pita bread.

Preheat the Airfryer to 390°F.

In a small bowl, stir together 1 teaspoon salt, the cumin, coriander, and red pepper flakes. Sprinkle the spice mixture evenly over the beef.

In a bowl, stir together the bell peppers, zucchini, summer squash, onion, oil, garlic, and cilantro. Season to taste with salt and black pepper.

Thread the meat and vegetables tightly onto the 4 skewers included with the double layer rack, alternating the pieces and dividing them evenly. Place the skewers on the rack and carefully set the rack inside the variety cooking basket. Insert the basket into the Airfryer. Cook, uncovered, until the vegetables are tender-crisp and the meat is medium-rare, 7–8 minutes.

Transfer the skewers to a platter and serve with lemon wedges, if desired.

SERVES 2

Kosher salt and freshly ground black pepper

½ teaspoon ground cumin

¼ teaspoon ground coriander

⅛ teaspoon red pepper flakes

½ lb boneless sirloin, cut into 1-inch cubes

½ red bell pepper, cut into 1-inch pieces

½ yellow bell pepper, cut into 1-inch pieces

1 small zucchini, cut into 1-inch pieces

1 small yellow summer squash, cut into 1-inch pieces

½ red onion, cut into 1-inch pieces

2 tablespoons olive oil

1 clove garlic, minced

2 teaspoons chopped fresh cilantro

Lemon wedges, for serving (optional)

Zucchini Fries

Here, panko bread crumbs are pressed onto pieces of zucchini and then airfried. The result is a deliciously crisp snack or appetizer that contains much less fat than traditional fried zucchini sticks. Serve these with aioli or your favorite good-quality ranch dressing.

Sprinkle the zucchini with salt and let stand at room temperature for 10 minutes.

Preheat the Airfryer to 390°F.

Gently blot the zucchini with paper towels to remove excess moisture. Place the zucchini in a large bowl, drizzle with the oil, and gently toss. Spread the panko on a plate. Roll the zucchini in the panko, coating all sides and pressing firmly so the crumbs adhere.

Working in batches, carefully place the zucchini in the variety cooking basket and insert the basket into the Airfryer. Cook, uncovered, turning the spears over halfway through cooking, until the zucchini is tender when pierced with a knife, about 7 minutes.

Transfer the zucchini to a platter and sprinkle with salt. Serve right away with aioli or ranch dressing.

SERVES 2–4

2 zucchini, about
1 lb total weight, cut into
2½-inch-long spears

Kosher salt

2 tablespoons olive oil

¾ cup panko bread crumbs

Aioli or ranch dressing,
for serving

Maple-Glazed Carrots

Roasting brings out the natural sweetness in carrots. Here, they're tossed with a maple glaze to create a delicious and healthy dish. Serve these alongside grilled chicken or steak, or let them cool and add them to a salad for a sweet surprise.

Preheat the Airfryer to 390°F.

In a bowl, toss together the carrots and melted butter. Carefully place half of the carrots on the nonstick grill pan and insert the pan into the Airfryer. Cook until the carrots are browned, about 10 minutes, gently shaking the pan halfway through cooking. Transfer to a bowl. Repeat with the remaining carrots.

Meanwhile, in a small saucepan over medium-high heat, combine the broth, thyme, and maple syrup. Bring to a boil and cook until reduced by half, about 5 minutes.

Add the maple glaze to the bowl with the carrots and toss to coat. Season to taste with salt and pepper and serve right away.

SERVES 2–4

1 lb carrots, peeled and cut on the bias into ½-inch rounds

1 tablespoon unsalted butter, melted

¼ cup chicken broth

½ teaspoon minced fresh thyme

2 tablespoons maple syrup

Kosher salt and freshly ground pepper

Spiced Potato Wedges

These crisp, smoky potato wedges make a tasty side dish as well as a snack. Serve them as is or with a side of garlic aioli if you are feeling a bit decadent. If you double the recipe, be sure to cook the potatoes in two batches.

Preheat the Airfryer to 390°F.

In a bowl, toss the potato with the oil until coated. In a small bowl, stir together ½ teaspoon salt, ⅛ teaspoon black pepper, the paprika, onion powder, garlic powder, and cayenne. Sprinkle the spice mixture over the potato and toss to combine.

Carefully place the potato wedges in the variety cooking basket and insert the basket into the Airfryer. Cook, uncovered, tossing and stirring them twice during cooking, until the wedges are crisp on the outside and tender on the inside when pierced with a knife tip, about 23 minutes.

Transfer the potatoes to a bowl and serve.

SERVES 2

1 russet potato, about ¾ lb, peeled and cut lengthwise into 8 wedges

1 tablespoon olive oil

Kosher salt and freshly ground black pepper

½ teaspoon smoked paprika

⅛ teaspoon onion powder

⅛ teaspoon garlic powder

Pinch of cayenne pepper

Pita Chips with Hummus

Be sure to use the thinner pocketed pita breads for this recipe, as pocketless ones are too thick to make into chips. These crispy chips are a snap to make and are just right for dipping into our creamy homemade hummus.

Preheat the Airfryer to 360°F.

To make the pita chips, brush the pita halves on both sides with the oil and sprinkle lightly with salt. Cut each pita half into 8 wedges. Carefully place half of the pita wedges in the variety cooking basket and insert the basket into the Airfryer. Cook, uncovered, carefully shaking the basket twice during cooking, until the wedges are crisp and golden, about 10 minutes. Transfer the chips to a baking sheet and let cool completely. Repeat with the remaining pita wedges.

Meanwhile, make the hummus: In a food processor, combine the chickpeas, tahini, garlic, lemon juice, oil, 1 tablespoon water, and salt to taste. Process until smooth, stopping occasionally to scrape down the sides of the bowl.

Transfer the hummus to a serving bowl, drizzle with oil, and sprinkle with paprika. Serve with the pita chips.

SERVES 4

For the pita chips

4 rounds pita bread, split in half horizontally along the seam

¼ cup olive oil

Kosher salt

For the hummus

1 can (15 oz) chickpeas, drained and rinsed

1 tablespoon tahini

1 small clove garlic, minced

2 tablespoons fresh lemon juice

2 tablespoons olive oil, plus more for drizzling

Kosher salt

Smoked paprika, for sprinkling

Jalapeño Poppers

Stuffed with corn kernels, crisp bacon, and Monterey jack cheese, these jalapeño poppers are the perfect appetizer for game day. You can make the stuffing and fill the jalapeños up to a day in advance, making these a quick and easy option for a gathering.

Preheat the Airfryer to 360°F.

In a sauté pan over medium heat, warm the oil. Add the onion and cook, stirring occasionally, until tender and translucent, about 6 minutes. Add the corn and cook, stirring occasionally, until soft, 2–3 minutes. Transfer to a bowl.

In the same pan over medium heat, cook the bacon until crisp and browned, 1–2 minutes.

Add half of the bacon to the corn mixture. Fold in the cheese and a pinch each of salt and pepper. Fill the jalapeño halves with the mixture, dividing evenly.

In a small bowl, stir together the remaining bacon and the panko. Sprinkle over the stuffed jalapeños.

Carefully place 4 jalapeño poppers in the variety cooking basket. Set the double layer rack inside the basket and place the remaining 4 poppers on the rack. Insert the basket into the Airfryer. Cook, uncovered, rotating them between the basket and rack halfway through cooking, until the poppers are crisp and lightly browned, about 10 minutes.

Transfer the jalapeño poppers to a platter. Season to taste with salt and pepper and serve right away.

SERVES 4

~~~~~~~~~~~~~~~~~~~~~~~~~~~

1 tablespoon olive oil

½ yellow onion, finely diced

¼ cup fresh or thawed frozen corn kernels

1 slice bacon, diced

1 cup shredded Monterey jack cheese

Kosher salt and freshly ground pepper

4 large jalapeño chiles, halved lengthwise, seeded, and deribbed

2 tablespoons panko bread crumbs

Kale Chips

Kale chips are a healthy and easy snack to make in the Airfryer. These are made simply with salt and black pepper, but feel free to experiment with different spices, like chili powder or coriander, to amp up the flavor of these addictive chips.

Preheat the Airfryer to 390°F.

In a large bowl, toss together the kale, oil, ½ teaspoon salt, and ¼ teaspoon pepper.

Working in batches, carefully place handfuls of the kale in the variety cooking basket and insert the basket into the Airfryer. Cook, covered, shaking the basket halfway through cooking, until the kale is crisp, about 5 minutes.

Transfer the chips to a bowl and season to taste with salt. Serve warm or at room temperature.

SERVES 2–4

1 bunch Tuscan kale, stemmed and leaves cut into 2-inch pieces

2 tablespoons olive oil

Kosher salt and freshly ground pepper

Samosas with Cilantro Sauce

Stuffed with tender potatoes and sweet peas and flavored with fragrant curry powder and garlic, these Indian-style treats are sure to be a hit at your next gathering. Airfrying puff pastry gives these samosas a crisp, flaky texture.

To make the samosas, in a large nonstick frying pan over medium-high heat, warm the oil. Add the onion and potato and cook, stirring occasionally, until tender, about 12 minutes. Add the peas, curry powder, garlic, and 1 teaspoon salt and cook, stirring constantly, for 1 minute. Transfer to a bowl.

Preheat the Airfryer to 390°F.

On a lightly floured surface, roll out the puff pastry into a 7-by-14-inch rectangle. Cut into 2 strips lengthwise, then into 4 sections crosswise to create 8 squares. Working with 1 pastry square at a time, lightly brush the edges with some of the egg wash. Spoon a scant 1 tablespoon potato mixture into the center. Fold the bottom right corner over to the top left corner, then press the edges with the tines of a fork to seal.

Carefully place 2 samosas in the variety cooking basket. Set the double layer rack inside the basket and place 2 samosas on the rack. Insert the basket into the Airfryer. Cook, uncovered, until the pastry is evenly browned, about 10 minutes. Transfer to a platter. Repeat with the remaining 4 samosas.

Meanwhile, make the cilantro sauce: In a mini food processor, combine the cilantro, garlic, ¾ teaspoon salt, the lemon juice, and oil and process until the mixture reaches a pesto-like consistency. Serve the sauce alongside the samosas.

SERVES 4

For the samosas

1 tablespoon vegetable oil

½ yellow onion, finely diced

1 cup finely diced peeled russet potato

½ cup thawed frozen peas

2 teaspoons curry powder

1 clove garlic, minced

Kosher salt

All-purpose flour, for dusting

1 frozen puff pastry sheet, thawed

1 large egg beaten with 1 teaspoon water

For the cilantro sauce

1 cup packed fresh cilantro leaves

1 small clove garlic, minced

Kosher salt

1 tablespoon fresh lemon juice

¼ cup olive oil

Spicy Chickpeas

Chickpeas, spiced with paprika and cumin, emerge crisp and exceptionally tasty when cooked in the Airfryer. To kick up the heat, add more cayenne pepper. Serve these as an afternoon pick-me-up, as a great accompaniment to a beer, or scatter them over a simple green salad.

Preheat the Airfryer to 390°F.

In a bowl, stir together the chickpeas, oil, paprika, cumin, 1 teaspoon salt, and the cayenne.

Carefully place the chickpeas in the variety cooking basket and insert the basket into the Airfryer. Cook, uncovered, carefully shaking the basket halfway through cooking, until the chickpeas are crisp, 8–10 minutes.

Transfer the chickpeas to a bowl and season to taste with salt. Serve warm or at room temperature.

SERVES 2–4

1 can (15 oz) chickpeas, drained and rinsed

1 tablespoon olive oil

1 teaspoon sweet paprika

½ teaspoon ground cumin

Kosher salt

Pinch of cayenne pepper

Cinnamon Apple Chips

Transform thinly sliced apples into the perfect snack in minutes using the Airfryer. Crisp and slightly chewy, these tart-sweet chips are lightly scented with cinnamon. They're a guaranteed kid-pleaser! Use an apple variety that holds its shape when cooked, such as Gala or Honeycrisp.

Preheat the Airfryer to 390°F.

Lay the apple slices on a baking sheet. In a small bowl, stir together the cinnamon, sugar, and a pinch of salt. Sprinkle the mixture over the apple slices.

Working in batches, carefully place the apple slices in the variety cooking basket and insert the basket into the Airfryer. Cook, uncovered, turning them over halfway through cooking, until the slices are lightly golden brown, 7–8 minutes.

Transfer the chips to a bowl and let cool before serving.

SERVES 2

1 apple, peeled and thinly sliced horizontally

½ teaspoon ground cinnamon

1 tablespoon sugar

Kosher salt

Triple-Chocolate Brownies

Made with chocolate chips, unsweetened chocolate, and cocoa powder, these dark chocolate treats will appease any chocolate lover. Add ¼ cup chopped toasted walnuts or pecans along with the chocolate chips, if you like. Serve these with your favorite ice cream or on their own.

Preheat the Airfryer to 330°F. Butter the bottom and sides of the nonstick baking dish.

In a small saucepan over low heat, combine the butter and chopped chocolate. Heat, stirring often, just until melted. Remove from the heat and let cool slightly. Stir in the cocoa powder.

In a large bowl, whisk together the eggs, sugar, salt, and vanilla until blended. Whisk in the melted chocolate mixture until completely blended. Add the flour and whisk just to incorporate, then fold in the chocolate chips.

Pour the batter into the prepared baking dish, spreading it evenly with a rubber spatula. Carefully place the baking dish in the variety cooking basket, cover with the splatter-proof lid, and insert the basket into the Airfryer. Bake until a toothpick inserted into the center of the brownies comes out with a few moist crumbs clinging to it, about 30 minutes.

Remove the baking dish from the Airfryer, place on a wire rack, and let the brownies cool completely in the dish. Invert the brownies onto a cutting board and flip right side up. Using a sharp knife, cut the brownies into squares and serve with vanilla ice cream, if desired.

SERVES 4

4 tablespoons unsalted butter, plus more for greasing

2 oz unsweetened chocolate, finely chopped

⅓ cup cocoa powder

2 large eggs

¾ cup sugar

¼ teaspoon table salt

½ teaspoon pure vanilla extract

½ cup all-purpose flour

½ cup chocolate chips

Vanilla ice cream, for serving (optional)

Index

THE AIRFRYER COOKBOOK

Conceived and produced by Weldon Owen, Inc.
In collaboration with Williams-Sonoma, Inc.
3250 Van Ness Avenue, San Francisco, CA 94109

A WELDON OWEN PRODUCTION
1045 Sansome Street, Suite 100
San Francisco, CA 94111
www.weldonowen.com

WELDON OWEN, INC.
President & Publisher Roger Shaw
SVP, Sales & Marketing Amy Kaneko
Finance Manager Philip Paulick

Associate Publisher Amy Marr
Associate Editor Emma Rudolph

Creative Director Kelly Booth
Art Director Marisa Kwek
Senior Production Designer Rachel Lopez Metzger

Printed and bound by 1010 Printing in China

Production Director Chris Hemesath
Associate Production Director Michelle Duggan

First printed in 2015
10 9 8 7 6 5 4 3

Photographer Aubrie Pick
Food Stylist Lillian Kang

Library of Congress Cataloging-in-Publication
data is available.

ISBN 13: 978-1-68188-016-7
ISBN 10: 1-68188-016-4

Weldon Owen is a division of **BONNIER**

ACKNOWLEDGMENTS

Weldon Owen wishes to thank the following people for their generous support
in producing this book: Amanda Anselmino, Kris Balloun, Ayesha Curry, Gloria Geller,
Bessma Khalaf, Kim Laidlaw, Jennifer Newens, Leigh Noe, and Elizabeth Parson